DETAILS

THE ARCHITECT'S ART

DETAILS

THE ARCHITECT'S ART

By Sally B. Woodbridge

Photographs by Roz Joseph

Chronicle Books • San Francisco

Printed in Hong Kong.

Library of Congress Cataloging in Publication Data

Woodbridge, Sally Byrne.
    Details: the architect's art / by Sally B. Woodbridge; photographs by
  Roz Joseph.
        p.   cm.
    Includes bibliographical references.
    ISBN: 0-87701-747-6 (pbk) ISBN: 0-87701-898-7 (cloth)
    1. Architecture—Details.   I. Joseph, Roz.   II. Title.
  NA2840.W66   1991
  721—dc20   90-43334
                                                        CIP

Editing: Judith Dunham
Book and cover design: Robin Weiss
Composition: On Line Typography
Illustrations: Diana Woodbridge

Distributed in Canada by Raincoast Books, 112 East Third Avenue
Vancouver, B.C., V5T 1C8

10 9 8 7 6 5 4 3 2 1

Chronicle Books
275 Fifth Street
San Francisco, California 94103

CONTENTS

WHY ORNAMENT?

Sally B. Woodbridge

Do buildings speak to us as we pass them on the street? If they do, what do they talk about, and what language are they using? This book seeks to answer those questions, to show how buildings communicate, or try to communicate, to passersby. For, like humans, buildings talk about themselves. Through the language of architectural detail or ornament, buildings reveal their character and their anatomy.

But what is architectural detail? The word *detail* has its root in the French verb *tailler*, "to cut," plus *de,* meaning "apart." Thus, details are small, secondary, or accessory parts of larger entities. Ornamental details such as wreaths, garlands of fruit and flowers, medallions with human heads, running bands of waves or chevrons, lion heads, scrolled leaves, and varieties of moldings do not occur randomly on buildings, but have a purpose. They mark the divisions into stories, define edges, and call attention to windows and doors.

In many ways, the design of buildings is analogous to that of clothing. The holes cut in cloth for the head, arms, and legs have always been opportunities for special treatment or decoration. The various approaches to cutting fabric, detailing seams, and finishing edges have helped to create distinctive styles. In both clothing and architecture, the pendulum of fashion swings back and forth between the lavishly ornamented and the stark and simple. One conclusion we might draw from this relentless tinkering is that humans are ornamenting animals.

1

Despite the many learned histories of architectural ornament that have been written, new theories about its origin and use continue to appear. No sooner does a consensus seem to exist that the purpose of ornament is and always was to express structure than other intriguing theories about the symbolic purposes of ornament arise. These theories suggest that an important role of ornament was to provide guidance on how people should lead their lives in harmony with the world of nature and the rhythms of the universe. That we should even expect such lessons from buildings seems incredible; yet before written language became a common tool of communication, buildings conveyed these messages through images carved on their walls in wood and stone.

Writing apparently evolved from pictures that represented things to signs that stood for sounds. Logos, short for logograms, are modern hieroglyphs. These easily assimilated visual symbols stand for words and are often more accessible within the memory than acronyms made of letters only. What, for instance, could be more compact and easy to read than the $ sign? Abstract concepts also have symbols; justice is commonly represented by a scale, and divine omniscience is portrayed by the all-seeing eye, a symbol that goes back to ancient Egypt at least, as is acknowledged on the one-dollar bill by emblazoning it on a pyramid.

Many of the motifs used in architectural detail are, like logos, highly compressed visual abstractions of ideas that would take up more space if they were fully explained. Even though, over time, many of the texts embellished by architectural detail lost their meaning, the motifs themselves survived because their forms were appealing. As pure ornament, these details composed a visual language that designers everywhere could use.

Today, public interest in buildings that display the kind of small-scale detail and texture provided by historic styles has increased to the point where architects are re-creating buildings from various periods with great attention to authentic detail. Reinterpreting historical detail for new buildings to make them harmonious with older settings is

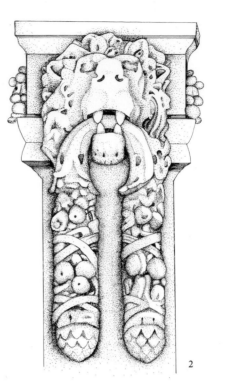

2

3

4

also a current concern. Whatever the circumstances, evidence abounds that the pendulum of fashion has swung away from the stark simplicity of architecture influenced by the revolt of the Modern Movement against the domination of history and tradition.

Although this new attitude toward the enrichment of buildings indicates a craving for complexity, it does not mean that we fully understand the purpose of architectural ornament. Does ornament express structure? Or is its main purpose to delight the senses? Or is there a deeper, more didactic purpose behind ornament that explains why buildings were adorned with humans, animals, flowers, fruit, and other odd elements, and seems to have nothing to do with the way buildings were constructed?

All three questions can be answered affirmatively, but much of the evidence is open to interpretation and, in fact, has been reinterpreted again and again. The intention of this book is not to write another learned history of architectural ornament, but rather to provide a context for looking at the subject in order to give the delightful fragments illustrated in these pages a larger meaning.

As shown by the photographs of architectural details in this book, most of the ornament that we see in American cities appears on nineteenth- and twentieth-century buildings designed in the so-called Classical style, which began, at least as we know it, in the fifth century B.C. So famous were temples such as the Parthenon that exemplified this style to those who saw them centuries later that they were copied wholly or partially throughout the Western world and even in Western-influenced parts of Asia. Since the interiors of temples were not used for public rituals and little was known of their appearance, the exterior was the most important aspect. They were rigorously studied in order to discover the rules that governed their harmonious composition, for

6

5

the exterior elements appeared to have been composed down to the smallest detail. If the building was in ruins, it could be reconstructed from fragments. Theories about order in Classical buildings were—and still are—being written in books and taught to architects.

Once understood, the temple was viewed as a kit of parts that could be taken anywhere. Why people wanted to take it home with them had to do with the fame of Greek civilization in the West, beginning in the Roman republic. Simply stated, the Romans used the older civilization to validate their new culture. The Romans grafted the Greek orders onto their new monuments, most notably the Colosseum, to advertise their authority. Centuries later, Thomas Jefferson used the temple to confirm the validity of the fledgling republican government of the United States. For the next century or so, Americans applied temple fronts to government buildings, banks, and other commercial buildings to promote confidence in their stability. Thus Classical architecture based on temple forms provided a marriage of eloquent structure and useful symbol. Yet, in the course of centuries of use, the Classical temple became such a familiar form that, like a log cabin, people recognized it without focusing on it in detail. When we look closely at the details on Classical buildings, we find them mysterious, perhaps even nonsensical. If the details are an integral part of the whole, then how did the whole come to be?

In his book, *The Lost Meaning of Classical Architecture,* George Hersey conjures up a vivid picture of the primordial temple as an altar set in a grove of trees, perhaps roped off to indicate a holy precinct. The trees were hung with the trappings of sacrifice, with the fruits and flowers of the harvest, and with the physical remains of sacrificial fowl and animals. According to Hersey, the latter were valued because they could be used to reassemble the victim and thereby turn the taking of life into a holy service. Thus, battle trophies composed of the slaughtered enemy's armor were exhibited not only as symbols of victory, but

Woodbridge '70

7

8

9

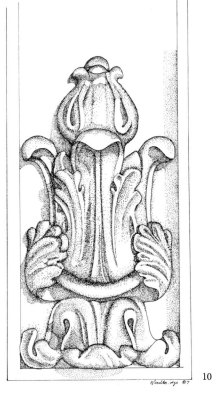

10

also as propitiation to the spirit of the deceased. Similarly, the bleached skulls of oxen, the beaks and claws of birds, and their many small bones were strung together on lines and displayed along with votive tablets and other paraphernalia used to invoke the divine presence.

The world of the ancient Greeks explored by Hersey was animistic. Moreover, the gods, who walked on earth in human form and meddled in human affairs, were also identified with trees: the oak with Zeus, the laurel with Apollo, the myrtle with Aphrodite, and so on. The appropriation of trees by the gods reflected, in turn, the status of the tree as a cosmic symbol: the *axis mundi,* or "world axis," that signified the central point of time and space and therefore of absolute reality. With its roots below ground and its branches lifted to the sky, the tree linked the earthly plane of human experience to the planes of the underworld and the heavens.

Tree worship did not originate with the Greeks; the concept of the *axis mundi* has been traced back to Neolithic times. In ancient China, as in ancient Greece, shrines to divinities were often placed at the roots of trees remarkable for their size and beauty, which were thought to house the divine essence. The cosmic Tree of Knowledge is a universal symbol that figured prominently in Judeo-Christian cosmology in the Garden of Eden. The tree is an essential component of paradise in Sumerian, Persian, Hindu, Chinese, and Japanese cultures. In the United States, we continue the originally pagan tradition of bringing trees into our houses and decorating them at Christmastime. Topping the tree with a star reinforces the significance of the tree as an *axis mundi* penetrating to the center of the earth and rising to the polar star.

Whereas the form of the Classical temple remained useful to Western civilizations, the religion that the temples honored did not. Why, then, were so many of the symbols of this archaic religion still used to adorn the Neo-Classical buildings in Europe and in the United States? One answer is that the details that originally had religious significance became aesthetically important. They were incorporated into the rules for architects and illustrated in the style manuals and pattern books without any attempt to explain their meaning.

12

"God is in the detail," Mies van der Rohe's famous utterance, means that, on one level, no matter what the size or importance of the building, its divine essence is revealed through structural expression. However, the simple or direct expression of how a building is put together is not what Mies had in mind. Rather it was the refinement of this prosaic expression into something poetic that concerned him.

The poetic expression of structure is not new. The ancient Greeks worked out an exquisite language of structural details that, according to some theories, served the purpose of memorializing the construction of the original wooden temples when longer-lasting stone became the preferred building material. The Roman architectural writer Vitruvius, from whom we derive most of our knowledge of Greek building practices, is an important source of this explanation for the form of the temple. Accordingly, the posts made from tree trunks became stone columns that supported the horizontal superstructure called an entablature, formerly a series of wood beams, which in turn supported the roof. The lack of arches in Greek temples would seem to indicate that the Greeks were not so much interested in the structural possibilities of stone over those of wood as they were in the durability of stone.

Some details of Greek temples relate directly to typical wood construction. For example, the frieze of the Doric temple is composed of alternating triglyphs and metopes. The three parts of the triglyph are thought to be wooden strips used to disguise the rough-cut ends of the ceiling beams. The Ionian temple has a series of dentils, teethlike elements, that might have been the ends of roof rafters in a wooden structure. Translated into stone and no longer of structural use, these motifs were valuable both as reminders of former construction and as elements that created a pattern of light and shadow that delighted the eye.

According to Vitruvius, the so-called Classical orders, or types, that comprised the columns and the entablature were named for their place of origin and the people who created them, the Dorians, the Ionians, and the Corinthians. But when we try to learn the reasons for the varied forms of these orders, we discover that myth and legend are at least as important as structure, if not more so, as in the case of the triglyph, which is only used in the Doric order.

In an essay titled "The Original Significance of the Model for the Doric Pteron and Triglyph," historian Goerd Peschken postulates that the form of the Doric temple echoes that of the raised corncribs found throughout the world wherever temperate climates necessitate the elevation of the harvested ears of corn off the damp ground and out of the reach of rodents. The survival of wood and stone corncribs in various parts of the world furnished Peschken with an opportunity to see corncribs in northern Portugal that have stone walls cut with slits very much like triglyphs. The cribs are raised on stone posts capped with disks that suggest the form of Doric capitals and functioned to foil the attempts of rodents to get to the stored corn.

The Doric temple appears with the rise of the Greek polis, or city-state, in the fifth century B.C. Peschken believes that in the transition from tribal to communal life, the Dorian clans decided to make a monumental version of their corncrib either to be used by the whole community or to commemorate past traditions of the clans. Theorists after Vitruvius who thought about the origin of the Doric temple hypothesized that the whole Doric entablature was a compressed, symbolic upper floor analogous to the barn lofts used for storing grain. If this kind of treasury was the original image of the temple, the broad use of the temple form for banks, mints, and other financial institutions seems more appropriate than ever.

13

The column capital also lends itself nicely to explanation in terms of structure. In order to diffuse the weight of the roof in the Greek temple, or in any post-and-lintel system, the top of the post was broadened or turned into a kind of cushion called a capital because it occurred at the head of the post. However it may once have functioned to prevent the ascent of rodents, the Doric capital also illustrates the principle of spreading the stresses of the roof's weight. The Corinthian capital has a more complicated form and another level of meaning that overlays the structural principle.

One interpretation of the Corinthian capital is based on the tale of a young maiden of the Greek city of Corinth who died before marriage and was duly buried. Her nurse gathered up some of her favorite possessions and put them in a basket, which she placed on the maiden's grave as a memorial. She covered the basket with a tile to weigh it down and keep out the rain. The nurse failed to notice that she had set the basket on top of an acanthus shoot, which, struggling to grow, curled its tendrils out from under the basket. In time the leaves unfolded around the base of the basket and beneath the tile lid. Who should be passing by but an architect, Callimachus, who was inspired to use the composition for a column capital. The only verifiable part of the legend is that Callimachus was a real person mentioned by the Roman writer Pliny and the Greek traveler Pausanias, and who built monuments in Corinth and was known for his bronze castings.

14

15

16

Neither the theory that trimmed tree trunks were used as columns in the early temple buildings nor that the peristyle came from the slotted walls of the corncrib can be proved, but the correspondences between trees and divinities in human form are striking. Hersey also discusses the possibility that real human beings may have been sacrificial victims lashed to the temple supports. Examining the literal meanings of the traditional architectural terms that signify the parts of the columns, he points out that, for example, the rounded torus and cavetto moldings on the column base in the Ionic and Corinthian orders derive their names from types of rope, which suggest the image of bound feet. Vitruvius compared the column flutes to the folds of the chiton, the common Greek dress in ancient times. The moldings at the top of the column shaft beneath the capital, called *trachelium* and *hypotrachelium*, come from the word for throat. Finally, the English word *capital* is derived from the Latin word for head. Following Hersey's lead, it is possible to see the leafy bands around Corinthian capitals as head bands or the volutes above as tightly coiled braids of hair.

17

18

19

As the orders and the rules for using them continued to evolve from Roman times through the Renaissance and into the eighteenth- and nineteenth-century revivals of Classicism, they were the focus of considerable invention that left the rules behind. Beyond the appearance of the orders lay the issues of the height and spacing between columns and other games of proportion on which architects spent much time and energy while studying architecture and designing buildings. The delight of eighteenth-century savants in the ruins of the ancient world, news of which poured in as curiosity and conquest took travelers and armies to far corners of the earth, produced many more theories on the origin and proper use of ornament.

The Greek orders were also related to humans by having a sex assigned to them. The Doric order was considered masculine because of its strength and simplicity. The more slender columns and the elaborate detail of the Ionic order made it feminine. The Corinthian order seemed to be sexless. This gender identification became impor-

tant when the question arose of what order to apply to a given building type. However, the theory that ornament should be suited to the use of the building and proportioned according to its location on the structure was strained in the eighteenth and nineteenth centuries both by the development of new building types and by the pleasure that designers took in inventing new ways to use the orders. What had been dogma became a question of fashion.

Today, we have ceased to turn to buildings to satisfy our need for imaginative experience; the advertising industry runs the symbol mills for which graphic designers still mine the past. But in our electronic age, the currents of meaning pass so quickly through images that if we want buildings to be up to the minute, we shall have to incorporate special effects into their basic palette of materials. If it is true that we are compulsive ornamenters, we will inevitably produce new vocabularies of architectural detail. After all, architecture is not only aesthetics put to use; it is a public utterance that tells us about ourselves.

HUMAN FORMS

Although humans have long been represented on buildings in cultures around the world, the human forms we find most often on buildings in American cities are based on Classical prototypes. The 1925 Exposition des Arts Decoratifs et Industriels in Paris, which included exhibits of decorative elements from all over the world, broadened the designer's frame of reference. Exotic vocabularies of ornament also gained attention through archaeological discoveries such as Tutankhamen's tomb in 1925 and the excavation of that time in Mesoamerica that revealed the complex and inscrutable Mayan art forms. Both Egyptian and Mayan reliefs rendered their subjects in more linear, less rounded forms than were used in the naturalistic Classical style. The popularity of these newly publicized styles influenced a shift in the way the human form was depicted in the arts and crafts of the 1920s and 1930s, as can be seen from the examples in this chapter. But no matter how human form was depicted, gods and mortals were differentiated by their symbols, not by their looks.

Setting aside public buildings occupied by government and cultural institutions, the most ornamented older buildings in American cities are devoted to commerce and finance. For these buildings the most popular deity was the Greco-Roman god, Hermes/Mercury, whose symbol, the caduceus (see page 62), often appears by itself.

The Greek god, Hermes, had several roles. As Zeus's messenger, he was equipped for his role with wings on his shoes and his hat. His symbol, the caduceus, indicated his ability to travel the *axis mundi,*

the cosmic axis around which all life revolves. He protected travelers, many of whom were traders, and thus became the god of commerce and profit, both legal and illegal. The Romans merged Hermes with the ancient Italic god of riches and profit, Mercurius, whose name was derived from *mercari,* which meant "to carry on a business."

In the frieze on the pediment above the entrance to this former Banca d'Italia (figure 22), Hera/Juno, the matriarch, holds the hands of Aphrodite/Venus and Hermes/Mercury, who is clad only in his winged hat and shoes, which are what made him superhuman. Both ends of the composition show the symbols of progress, the train and the ship that brought prosperity to San Francisco. They are appropriate because the Banca d'Italia, which later became the Bank of America, was founded in San Francisco. The other relief of Hermes/Mercury is executed in a different style. Figure 23 shows the influence of Egyptian or Assyrian art.

23

The Roman god of healing, Aesculapius, was introduced in Rome during a plague in 293 B.C. and became increasingly popular thereafter. Emperor Marcus Aurelius even had himself represented as Aesculapius holding a caduceus (figure 24). The twin snakes represented the opposing forces of health and sickness; healing was achieved through a balance of these and other opposites. It is easy to confuse these gods; the inclusion of a chemist's vial in this relief identifies the character as Aesculapius.

This character may be Pan, shown tripping along playing his pipes and accompanied by a wild beast (figure 25). If so, the artist has chosen to give him human legs instead of the goat legs he usually has, but he still has the horns and tail that identify him as a nature god. Although horns are usually interpreted as links to the bestial world, they may also be seen as rays of the sun and signs of divine knowledge and power. Pan is probably depicted here because of his musical talent—many a nymph danced to the tune of his pipes.

Terpsichore is the muse of dance and music, shown here plucking her lyre, but not seeming too happy about whatever she hears (figure 26). Both Pan and Terpsichore look as though they were modeled from real people rather than from book illustrations of Classical figures.

In another, more ancient guise, Hermes was honored by the Greek shepherds of Arcadia who invoked his protection by piling up stones outside their houses as resting places for his spirit. In time, these heaps of stones marked routes for travelers and evolved into steles, or stone shafts, capped with Hermes's head. A link appears to have existed between the herms, as they were called, and the anonymous humans that appear on buildings as columnlike supports. These creatures, also called atlantes and caryatids, have heads and torsos, but at their midsections they turn into architectural elements. Although all three characters play the same role, they came to it in different ways.

24

25

26

27

28

Atlantes are related to Atlas, the Titan who was sentenced to support the heavens because he joined in a revolt against the gods. *Atlantes* is one name for the muscular, weary-looking men bowed down by the weight of cornices, balconies, etc. They are also called herms, perhaps as a result of incorporating this protecting effigy into the building.

Freestanding sculptures that hold up parts of buildings can be traced to legends surrounding the caryatids, the six statues of women that support the roof of the porch, sometimes called "the porch of the maidens," of a building of mysterious use called the Erechtheum,

29

30

which stands on the Acropolis in Athens. Vitruvius wrote that the human columns commemorated the punishment of the women of the town of Caryae (*caryatid* translates as "resident of Caryae") who with their husbands conspired to help the invading Persians defeat the Greeks. After the defeat of the Persians, the Greeks killed the men of Caryae and took the women to Athens as captives, where they were displayed weighted down as punishment for their sins. Turning these women into a permanent moral lesson, if indeed that was the intention behind the sculptures, failed, as have many moral lessons in stone.

Although the original caryatids do not seem to be suffering, most other humans who appear in supporting roles in buildings have the distorted faces and contorted postures to be expected from bearing such a painful and permanent burden. Whatever the origin of this enslavement of humans to architecture, the public exhibition of prisoners of war and other miscreants bound or chained to structures was a common practice in many cultures.

Malevolent spirits permanently subdued by architectural bondage are common on buildings that use a medieval vocabulary of ornament. Ironically, these grimacing figures cannot be taken seriously; their stony pain seems droll.

Several kinds of detached heads appear on Classical buildings on the keystones of arches, gazing out from under balconies and roofs, or festooned with foliage on friezes. These heads are usually bearded males with long curling locks that merge into plant tendrils. This category of ornament has long been labeled "grotesque" and is commonly used to describe something that is distorted or twisted out of its natural state.

The root of the word *grotesque* is *grotta,* or *grotto. Grotta,* in turn, comes from the Latin word *grupta* or *crypta, krypte* in Greek, which referred to an underground passage or cave. Starting with this clue, we might reason that grotesques are copies of mythical, freakish creatures with which the ancient Greeks and Romans decorated caves and sea grottoes. However, the origin of the grotesque appears to lie not in ancient customs, but in a misunderstanding of ancient ruins. In the excavations of Roman ruins, particularly of Emperor Nero's Golden House on the Esquiline Hill that was carried out in 1488, wall paintings of fantastic creatures and foliage were found in rooms that were underground because subsequent layers of buildings had covered them. The paintings inspired a form of decoration called grotesque because the buried rooms were assumed to be caves.

31

33

32

34

To complicate the issue, the Romans constructed artificial grottoes, which were used as prototypes for those made during the Renaissance in such famous gardens as the Boboli. The idea spread throughout Europe in the sixteenth and seventeenth centuries and to England in the Classical Revival of the eighteenth century. The printing press facilitated the dissemination of images of grotesques in response to a demand for titillating exotica that had only the most tenuous connection to monsters that may have lurked in grottoes.

Classical male and female heads were fashioned after traditional representations of gods, goddesses, heroes, and the typically female personifications of virtues such as justice and truth. Bearded male heads with long tangled locks of hair and fierce expressions may be Titans, the secondary race of gods spawned by Uranus and Gaea, who were giants and therefore capable of bearing heavy loads.

36

35

37

Female heads, sometimes with torsos, bearing garlands of fruit and flowers, were popular even for office buildings, despite the absence of any ties between the rural celebrations of the seasons and the bounty of agriculture and the urban world of getting and spending. Still, symbolic representations of fertility to ensure abundance are beneficial for any endeavor. Whatever their provenance, human heads were surely intended to humanize buildings as well as bring good fortune. Though unidentified, these heads often escape being mere types and remind us that they must have been modeled after real people, friends no doubt of the architects and artisans who made them.

39

40

38

41

42

43

Figure 43 shows a weary-looking young woman shouldering a heavy yoke of fruits of the field. She represents one of the four seasons, but it is unclear which one since the other maidens also have garlands of fruits and flowers. Still, prosperity and abundance are the most common symbols for buildings of finance and commerce. This plaque is part of the array of architectural detail in terra cotta that was produced for the 1926 Hunter-Dulin building by Gladding, McBean, whose work is more fully discussed on pages 63–67.

The muscular woman raising her arm to let the miniature steam engine pass underneath is rendered in the geometric style of Art Deco that was used in the design of the Pacific Stock Exchange Club of 1930 by Miller and Pflueger (figure 44). The angular emphasis of this style even affected the shape of the medallion, which is polygonal instead of round as in the plaque on the Hunter-Dulin building. The emblematic use of transportation and other man-made energy systems was also a mark of modern times. Humankind's dedication to unleashing nature's energy was often portrayed by rendering people as embodiments of energy. The figures flanking this entrance merge with the radiating lines of energy that they strain to harness or release (figure 45).

44

45

Real people were certainly the models for the figures representing, on the far right, the production of electrical energy, and, below, its application. These symbolic figures appear on either side of the Pacific Gas and Electric Company sign atop the arched entrance to its 1925 office building in San Francisco. The whole composition, which also shows a model powerhouse centered on top of the sign, exemplifies the formerly common practice whereby corporate entities integrated into their buildings monumental compositions with appropriate symbolic detail that proclaimed their ownership to passersby. Sculptor Edgar Walter was well known, as were the architects, Bakewell and Brown.

46

The female figure (figure 47) was designed by Bernard Maybeck, who delighted in transforming canonical forms to suit his own purposes. Here he reversed the traditional pose of the female caryatid for the Palace of Fine Arts, which he designed for the 1915 Panama-Pacific International Exposition in San Francisco. Instead of facing outward, Maybeck's women turn their backs on the world and appear to be brooding into coffinlike planters that never contained plants. By his own account, Maybeck thought that the fine arts had a melancholy tone and designed the draped women and the monumental urns to create a pensive mood.

47

48

ANIMAL AND  BIRD FORMS

nimals have generally accompanied humans and, in the case of those commonly depicted on buildings, were represented because they exemplified desirable character traits. The majestic lion, sign of the zodiac and symbol of the sun and its powers, was associated with authority in many cultures. The lion is a good example of an exotic beast that many people recognized, even before the advent of public zoos, because of its representation on public buildings.

The lion and the unicorn that stand on either side of the clock above the entrance to the former, London-based Royal Globe Insur-ance Company of 1907 come from the British coat of arms (figures 50 and 51). The solar majesty of the lion is paired with the lunar purity of the unicorn to signify the union of opposites. This union was also symbolized by the single horn of the unicorn, which stood for purity and accounts for the unicorn's association with the Virgin Mary and with monastic life. This mythical beast, occurring in Egyptian, Greco-Roman, Hebrew, Sumero-Semitic, and Chinese cosmologies, has the head and body of a horse, the tail of a lion, the legs and hoofs of a stag, and a twisted horn in the center of its forehead.

49

50

51

The ram, another sun symbol, appears in many cultures. As Aries, the first sign of the zodiac, the ram symbolized the beginning of any cycle or process of creation. As a symbol of the masculine generative force, the ram was preeminently a sacrificial animal; its horns signified honor, solar and lunar power, and abundance. The ram shown below, a High Sierra bighorn sheep, looks over the branch of a California live oak on the walls of the Pacific Gas and Electric Company building in San Francisco.

The bull and the ox share many attributes and were both sacrificed during the rituals of the harvest to ensure the renewal of the earth and earthly powers. The skulls of oxen, called bucrania, were carved on the friezes of Doric temples. Bedecked with garlands of fruit and flowers, the skulls doubtless replicated the real sacrificial offerings that were hung on the temples during the seasonal rites. These images continued to appear well into the twentieth century. One wonders whether they were consciously used as puns on buildings dedicated to the rituals of finance or whether the designers were simply following the rules for the composition of the orders.

52

53

The grizzly bear is one of California's state symbols. Representations of the bear hardly convey its ferocity when aroused, but its power is at least suggested in the medallion in which the bear appears stepping over the skyline of San Francisco (figure 54).

Beneath the heraldic sign on the Pacific Gas and Electric building, a worried-looking bear peers down through sheaves of grain and garlands of fruit, all symbolizing California (figure 55). It is hard to imagine a real grizzly in this demeaning situation.

The two heraldic bears holding the monogram of the Banca d'Italia also look a bit silly, but this use of native animals shows the importance that financial enterprises once attached to a particular locale (figure 56).

An affable bear sits placidly atop his column in front of a former Cadillac showroom (figure 57). Doubtless he posed for this portrait in his den at the zoo rather than in the wild.

54

55

56

57

Hilgard Hall, a Department of Agriculture building on the University of California campus at Berkeley, is lavishly decorated with friezes that celebrate the rewards of tilling the earth and also depict familiar barnyard animals. The honored creatures, here the horse and the rooster, appear in framed portraits hung above massive garlands of produce that hang from candelabra (figures 58 and 59). The technique used is sgraffito, taken literally from the Italian verb *sgraffire,* "to scratch." In sgraffito work, whether in ceramic or in plaster, two coats of contrasting colors are applied and the top coat is scratched through to create a very shallow relief with a colored background.

59

ANIMAL AND BIRD FORMS

60

61

62

If the lion is the king of the beasts, the eagle has the same status in the realm of birds. Because of its power to fly to great heights, the eagle was thought to have godly vision and, as Zeus's bird, to be at home with thunder and lightning, war and power. The choice of the native bald eagle as the national symbol of the United States was also effective in identifying the government with the sources of Western civilization in the ancient Greco-Roman world. In Chinese and Indian art, the eagle may have been one source for the mythic garuda, a celestial bird that is often shown fighting.

Regardless of their high standing, eagles have not escaped the vagaries of fashion. In figure 60 and figure 61, they are portrayed abstractly and realistically, depending upon whether the buildings they appear on are Classical or Moderne. Although stationary, they are never at rest. Ever poised for flight, they stand with their mighty wings half or fully unfurled.

Another legendary bird about the size of an eagle but with some features of the pheasant is the phoenix. According to the legend, when the phoenix sensed the approach of death, it would make a nest for itself of scented resinous wood and expose it to the full rays of the sun with the result that bird and nest were totally consumed by fire. This act of self-immolation produced another phoenix born of the marrow of the charred bones. As a symbol of renewal and resurrection, the phoenix existed in many cultures. For the Aztecs, Mayans, and Toltecs, the phoenix was the quetzal; for the Chinese, the phoenix, or the fenghuang, was the emperor of birds and was associated with that other imperial symbol, the dragon. The Egyptian phoenix, the bennu, was a sun bird associated with Ra. A useful symbol in modern times, the phoenix was adopted by San Francisco following the destruction of much of the city by the earthquake and fire of 1906.

63

64

65

66

This phoenix rises from its ashes holding a flowering branch, a sign of renewal, in its beak (figure 63). The bird is framed in an elegant cartouche set below the imposing lion-and-unicorn sign of the former Royal Globe Insurance Company. The company's building was constructed just after the 1906 earthquake and fire, from which San Francisco rose from the ashes.

A most unflattering image of the phoenix shows a bird with knobby knees, its wings flattened against the wall as it bends over holding a ring in its beak for some mysterious reason (figure 64). The pink paint is doubly insulting.

If the eagle was the bird of light, the owl (figure 65) was associated with the death of the sun and the dark powers of the underworld. Athena is often accompanied by an owl and was at times described as owl-eyed, which may suggest an earlier version of this ancient goddess in the shape of an owl. In any case, the owl, like Athena/Minerva, was also associated with wisdom.

Doves, favored as symbols of peace in Classical times, were often shown carrying sprigs of olive, another symbol of peace. As votive birds, they were kept in temple precincts and sacrificed in ritual offerings. Their eggs were also used in rituals and symbolized, as did all eggs, the world egg, one of mankind's oldest symbols for the germ of creation. In Christian iconography, the dove symbolizes the Holy Spirit and is often depicted in a posture of descent to suggest the flow of grace from heaven to earth. In general, birds symbolized the celestial world. Winged humans may be celestial because they dwell in the sight of God, as in the case of angels (of which the Bible names nine orders, each with a different number of wings), or because they are capable of becoming airborne like Hermes/Mercury, which made them superhuman but not necessarily angelic. Speed, another message of wings, is advertised by this winged wheel (figure 66).

67

The dolphin, like the anchor with which it is often shown, is a symbol of salvation, a sea creature friendly to humans and a saviour of the shipwrecked. Dolphins are favorite symbols of maritime enterprises and seaport cities. Sometimes the speedy dolphins are entwined with an anchor, symbolizing prudence or hastiness held in check. Often they are shown with a seashell, which, by itself, is a typical symbol of the sea and of birth.

68

Sea lions are an attraction for tourists who watch their activities on the rocky offshore islands in the Pacific Ocean. The sea lions flanking this portrait of a clipper ship effectively conveyed the nature of Hippolyte Audiffred's trading company established in San Francisco in the mid-nineteenth century. The single sea lion, below, poses as a San Francisco mascot holding a shield.

The walrus head was one of a row of such heads that adorned the Alaska Building, demolished in the 1970s. Appropriately, the walrus wears a halo of rope and a long-suffering expression (figure 71).

69

70

71

73

Although related to the dragons that ripple across the roofs of buildings in Chinatown, the winged dragon about to take flight from the corner of this building is of a different style (figure 72). Much diminished in recent times, the power of the dragon in China made its representation a staple motif on clothing, articles of ceremonial and everyday use, and architecture, including garden walls where its serpentine form was rendered in tile work capping the wall. The Chinese recognized nine kinds of dragons, including the Celestial Dragon, protector of the mansion of the gods; the Spiritual Dragon, producer of wind and rain; and the Winged, the Horned, and the Coiling dragons. From the Han to the Ching dynasties (206 B.C.–A.D. 1912), the imperial coat of arms featured two dragons fighting for a pearl, variously interpreted as the sun, the moon, or the world egg.

The broad array of running motifs that includes waves, spirals, coils, plaits, zigzags, chevrons, and frets, or Greek keys, share a use of serpentine forms that, like dragons, are symbols of the activity of the natural forces, earth, fire, air, and water. Appropriately, these motifs are often used to unify architectural compositions.

74

HERALDRY AND EMBLEMS

Company logos have taken the place of the heraldic crests emblazoned on shields that used to proclaim the lineage of firms belonging to the aristocracy of business and commerce. It is interesting to observe how designers addressed this need for status in the days when corporations put their stamp on buildings that they thought they would occupy permanently, in contrast to the short-term stake that most now have in the buildings where their offices are located. The examples shown here of the Matson Steamship Lines and the Pacific Telephone Building are notable because of the attention given to personalizing them. The "M" for Matson on page 71 is rendered in rope, and the whole building is detailed with nautical symbols such as anchors, dolphins, and shells. Portraits of Matson steamships also appear in cartouches.

For the Pacific Telephone Building on page 64, a polychromed blue and white bell, modeled by Gladding, McBean sculptor Pio Oscar Tognelli, is framed in a rondel hung above stafflike elements that were often used as symbols of authority.

The portrait of a chair on page 65 is one of several that appear on the Breuner Building in Oakland to celebrate founder John Breuner's career as a furniture manufacturer.

The decorative details for these buildings were executed by Gladding, McBean in Lincoln, California, the terra-cotta manufacturing company that, since 1875, produced terra-cotta ornament for a large number of buildings, particularly on the west coast.

The choice of Lincoln for the factory site followed the discovery nearby of an extensive deposit of pure white kaolin clay, which partners

Charles Gladding, Peter McGill McBean, and George Chambers leased from its owner George Towle in 1875 for the production of vitrified sewer pipe. The product had a bright future because of the dramatic growth of west coast cities in the latter part of the nineteenth century. In 1884, the company began to make architectural ornament and, to advertise itself, built a two-story company headquarters building, long gone, at 1358 Market Street in San Francisco.

Architectural terra cotta was less expensive than stone and could be glazed and textured to mimic different kinds of the more costly material, from warm, buff-colored sandstone to cool, gray granite. Terra cotta was also lighter and saved money by reducing the amount of structural steel needed for the building frame. Architects favored the material because their designs could be modeled at full scale and reworked, if necessary, before they were cast. Despite the need for skilled labor to make the molds, they could be reused more or less indefinitely. The standardization provided by the use of molds guar-

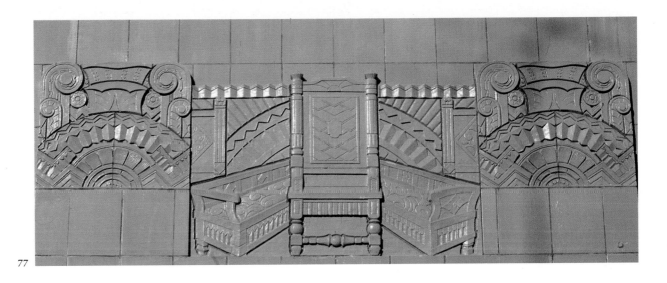

anteed accuracy in repeated ornament, saved money through speedy execution, and avoided the need for expensive skilled labor for site work. To reduce costs further, it was common practice to construct tall buildings using stone on the ground floor and perhaps on the second and third floors, if they were very visible from the street. But the upper floors were more often clad in terra cotta or cast stone colored and textured to imitate whatever stone was used below.

Shapes of Clay, a company publication, described the process by which an architect's drawing was turned into reality. In the factory drafting room, the drawing was keyed to show the location of the terra-cotta ornament. Then, a shop drawing was made following the architect's drawing and submitted to the architect for approval. Next, working drawings were made in full size with allowance for shrinkage, and every piece was scheduled. At the factory, staff artists modeled the ornament in clay and plaster. After approval by the architect—often through a review of photographs taken in the shop—the model was

78

sent to the plaster shop where final molds were made. The publication noted the creative efforts of the staff sculptors, but added that they were always under the supervision of the architect. Architects also commissioned artists not employed by Gladding, McBean to execute certain work. The 1989 monograph, *Architectural Terra Cotta of Gladding, McBean*, by Gary F. Kurutz with photographs by Mary Swisher, offers a detailed account of the company's history with descriptions of the production of architectural terra cotta and anecdotes about the company's experience working with well-known architects who designed many of the flagship buildings for San Francisco, Oakland, Sacramento, and other cities in the state and around the country.

A wreath flanked by candelabra surrounds a helmet, an axe, and a bell, the fireman's attributes, which adorn a spandrel of the former Fireman's Fund Insurance building in San Francisco (figure 78).

The scrolled foliage supporting a crown is the kind of all-purpose crest that anyone could use and understand. But the plumed shield bearing dolphins entwining a trident with fleurs-de-lis on either side is difficult to decipher (figures 79 and 80).

79

80

These reliefs of what appear to be stacks of urns, each with a round shield bearing a rosette in the middle, are cryptic to modern eyes (figures 81 and 82). They are probably trophies, not of the military kind that featured armor and other weapons, but perhaps related to military trophies if the urns held treasure and other spoils of battle. Such representations of treasure trophies were created in the Renaissance to advertise the achievement of wealth. Trophies are still given for achievement in sports and other contests, but the practice of displaying treasure trophies on the walls of financial institutions, as was the case in the Roaring Twenties when this building was designed, has been abandoned in favor of announcing wealth and the security it inspires by means of luxurious materials and monumental scale.

Heraldry appeared throughout Europe in the twelfth century and was used to proclaim the importance of feudal families. Human heralds were officials whose duties were to conduct royal ceremonies. From medieval times on, heraldry was mainly concerned with family genealogies and devising coats of arms. In times of great social mobility, the demand for such emblems of respectability increased. Even companies and corporations adopted heraldic devices to proclaim their importance. Heraldic ornament designed for buildings tended to be prominently displayed on entrances, but miscellaneous emblems such as shields and scrolls were often used simply to enliven walls or fill empty spaces. These two relief panels are set between windows. Both bear blank shields and scrolls, for, as was often the case, these are anonymous symbols of fame. The relief, figure 83, has stacks of urns that recall the treasure trophies in the preceding illustrations. In figure 84 the shield is flanked by torches, emblems of honor.

81

82

83

84

Symbols derived from the rituals of fraternal organizations are sometimes easy to understand and sometimes obscure. Figure 85 depicts various symbols used by the Independent Order of Odd Fellows (IOOF), which was founded in the eighteenth century in Manchester, England, as a benevolent secret society. Odd Fellows were not odd in the sense of being eccentric; rather, they were out of place or far from home. In 1819, the organization spread to the United States, where many chapters were founded to help strangers, odd fellows, find companionship and assistance in managing their lives. The organization boomed in California with the mass migration during the Gold Rush of 1849. Nearly every town had a building owned by the IOOF, which usually had commercial uses on the lower floors and a meeting hall for the society on an upper floor. The secret part of the society was its rituals, to which only members were privy and which borrowed from the rituals of the Masonic Order and the Rosicrucians. Egyptian esoterica was one source of symbols. At the top of this relief panel is the all-seeing eye ringed with sun rays above the new moon and stars symbolizing enlightenment, but perhaps containing other hidden meanings. The links of chain above clasped hands no doubt symbolize brotherhood. At the bottom of the panel is a tent of the kind used in the deserts of Egypt. A tent with an open flap generally alludes to the passage of the soul from one world to another and, in this case, is an enigmatic symbol. However, the image is not illogical, for one of the important roles of the IOOF was to take charge of burying those members who died far from home without family ties.

PLANT  FORMS

Until the late nineteenth century when the industrial revolution began to focus attention on the machine, designers drew their major inspiration for the forms of architectural ornament from nature. Ancient civilizations in all parts of the world deified nature. Not only did the Christian world consider nature a mirror of the divine order, but even the rationalist period of the Enlightenment in Europe found an order in nature that was not susceptible to improvement by mankind.

Although a great debate raged in the nineteenth century about the use of nature in architectural ornament, the issue was not whether ornament should follow nature, but how faithfully natural forms should be rendered. Should the flowers and foliage be so realistic that they appeared to grow on the building, or should they express in a more abstract way the structural elements with which they were associated?

A swing between realism and abstraction has marked the history of the representation of plant forms in architectural ornament. Although Egyptian ornament that features the lotus and papyrus and other vegetation appears quite stylized when compared with Hellenic and Hellenistic Greek versions of flowers and foliage, Egyptian plant forms are more realistic than the very abstract motifs of Islamic art. This intricate and stylized interlacing of flowers and foliage with geometric elements was distinctive enough to merit its own name, *arabesque,* signifying an Islamic or Arabian origin.

87

Representations of God or humans were forbidden by Mohammed, but natural forms and geometry were permitted and even used as aids to meditation. They were woven into a network that symbolized cosmic activity and a progressive reconciliation of opposites through graduated and repeated motifs. Arabesques, derived from the inlaid metalwork produced in Persia and Syria, were particularly fashionable in Europe from the mid-sixteenth to the early seventeenth century. Moslem craftsmen working in Venice at the end of the fifteenth century may have initiated the vogue. Combinations of arabesque and strap work, so-called because it resembled the twisted and intertwined leather straps or ribbons that evolved in northern Europe in the sixteenth century, ensued and were worked to extreme in the nineteenth-century eclectic revivals that dissolved all geographic and cultural boundaries.

The endlessly repeated species of flowers and trees were native to the lands that had spawned the major vocabularies of natural ornament. The frond of the palm tree, which flourished in so much of the ancient world and symbolized victory and honor, was a staple motif of many ancient cultures. In the stylized form it achieved in the Greco-Roman system, the palmette was almost interchangeable with the anthemion, which was derived from either the honeysuckle or the acanthus flower or perhaps from another, older plant sacred to the Egyptians or ancient Persians.

The evergreen laurel or bay tree signified honor and glory as well as renewal and resurrection. The leaves were woven into wreaths and crowns or bound into ropes sometimes with the berries and used as garlands and festoons. Oak and olive leaves served the same purpose in ceremonies honoring athletes and military heroes. The simple, generic shapes of laurel and olive leaves made them useful in combination with other plant forms. The oak leaf and acorn were more complex forms, but not so complex as the acanthus leaf, which is by far the most ubiquitous plant in the Classical vocabulary of ornament.

88

89

90

A sheaf of wheat is enshrined on one of the panels of Hilgard Hall on the campus of the University of California in Berkeley (figure 90). On the window spandrel of the building, the same wheat is flanked by winnowing baskets that resemble straw hats, behind which are a pair of crossed flails that were used to thresh the grain by hand to separate the chaff from the kernels.

Another interesting use of plant forms appears on the tower of this Queen Anne house that has a wide band studded with oversized posies that have the look of Pop Art (figure 92).

94

The decorative detail of the Oakland City Hall was designed in 1911 by the New York architects Palmer and Hornbostel, who contracted with M. R. Giusti of New York to create models for almost all the ornament. The models were shipped to the Gladding, McBean plant in Lincoln, California, where they were cast. Although the main cladding is stone, all the detail is in creamy terra cotta. The light standards at the entrance have grapes, pinecones, and acanthus leaves; the frieze above the first story has California grapes, olives, and figs suspended from a running scroll of volutes (figure 93). Both the color and the elaborate detail contribute to the wedding cake quality of the building.

Among flowers, the rose has been a ubiquitous and recurrent symbol in Oriental and Occidental culture. Perfection and completion are perhaps the most universal meanings of the rose, but other meanings that indicate a resolution of opposites are time and eternity, life and death, fertility and virginity. The mystic rose corresponds to the lotus in Oriental culture; both flowers have different shades of meaning depending on the number and color of petals they are given. The architectural ornament called a rosette may indeed be a rose, but the form—a flower viewed frontally with a center and many petals—could easily ·be some other species. The rosette is valuable for its versatility. Like wreaths or the simple circular forms called pies—no relation to the edible kind—modeled after the Chinese circles that symbolize the heavens, these circular motifs can be used in a series or singly. Bosses in the form of rosettes, also called *paterae*, have been used to cover bolts, nails, and awkward joinery (see drawing on page 9). In these functional situations, the flower may not have had a symbolic role per se. As with the lily, which was transformed into a trefoil and quatrefoil, the decorative possibilities of the form ultimately became more important than the esoteric meaning.

93

Building Tops, 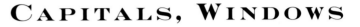 Capitals, Windows and Doors

Whether we are discussing a garment or a building, the incisions made in its fabric for arms and legs or windows and doors require attention. Since people are mobile, the bottoms of garments must be finished in some way; they cannot be left to unravel and trip the wearer. Although buildings are not mobile, they reach skyward. As in garments, the tops need finishing. Although the aesthetics of building tops have changed periodically, civic pride in a dramatic skyline has dictated much of the concern for having well-mannered, often memorable, and at times spectacular building tops.

The tops of tall buildings that give character to a city skyline are not the only ones that have received special treatment. The rooftops of late-nineteenth-century houses and parapets of 1920s and 1930s commercial buildings are among the most decorated parts of buildings. The triangular ends of the gable roofs of houses may not have windows if unused attic space exists behind them. In this case, the triangular space may be filled with decorative plasterwork in panels or an allover motif. But if the attic had usable space, windows were added. Square or rectangular windows created more triangular panels around them. This division of surfaces into large and small panels is characteristic of both exterior and interior surface treatment in Victorian houses. Not only were panels infilled with a variety of naturalistic or geometric motifs — the house in figure 96 has scrolling vines, fantastic beasts, suns, and circles inscribed with rays — but the whole was framed in a series of moldings and running motifs such as dentils. This concern for composing every inch of space often had the effect of trussing up a facade so that none of its parts could stray out of the visible frame.

95

Any aesthetic that has the strength to grip the whole of society for a decade or so leaves its imprint on every article of use. Thus, in the Victorian era, multiple trimmings also occurred in clothing and household appointments such as window drapes, furniture upholstery, carpets, and bedspreads and linens. Furniture design often echoed architecture with exaggerated scale given to the heads of beds, mantlepieces, and cabinets for china and dinnerware.

As we have now had time to observe, the Victorians' horror of blank space caused a severe reaction in the Modernists, who set about purging buildings of such unneeded decoration. But by now, the pendulum of fashion has reversed its direction again, and we find the seemingly endless variations of late-nineteenth-century themes of decoration quite delightful.

Parapets, those false fronts that cap the top of the streetfront, were a likely place for decorative detail because their main function was to provide a finished edge for the facade by hiding the true shape of the building's roof. The stylized geometric ornament of circles, spirals, chevrons, etc., used on Art Deco buildings lent itself to repetition in panels of cast plaster or terra cotta that were a relatively inexpensive way of enriching parapets. Volutes, which had been used in Classical detail, were particularly popular. They could be interpreted as unfurling plant forms or as the curling crests of waves, depending on whether they were used vertically or horizontally. The Art Deco–style building top is capped with a series of volutes and framed with pilasters that burst into bloom at the top (figure 99). In the center is a spray of volutes that suggests either a fountain or an exotic bouquet, and which bears the insignia of an organization called the Woodmen of the World, owner of the building.

96

97

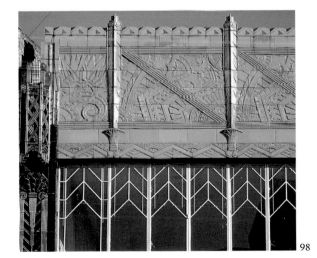

98

99

100

The range of designs for capitals shown on this page indicates how varied their forms could be. Although some of them are clearly based on the Classical Ionic and Corinthian orders, they are far from pure and simple specimens. The practice of adding extra leaves and garlands or festoons to the basic composition of the Classical orders was common from the sixteenth century on, whereas the revivals of Byzantine, Arabic, Romanesque, and other historic systems of ornament contributed exotic animal and bird forms. Human heads peer out of foliage on some capitals, recalling the legendary origin of columns in trees that were home to nymphs and gods. Perhaps the architects viewed the design of these no longer structural elements as a kind of creative doodling.

102

101

103

104

Like columns and capitals, windows and doors are often elaborated well beyond their basic functions. Although the style of a building somewhat determined the choice of decorative detail for windows and doors, how much or how little decoration was applied to the area around the opening was still a matter of some choice.

Unlike doors, windows have aprons, which are the panels below their sills, and these offer an additional space for ornament. Windows are often tied together, if they occur serially, by friezes or other kinds of running detail. Or, as can be seen in figure 105, simple repetition of windows along a stair is effective in itself. Even when window frames are simple, their glass may be enriched with color or etched with patterns. The mullions or muntins that hold the panes of glass may form geometric patterns in metal. Lavishly ornamented metal grills and screens also enrich doors and windows.

A grand entrance has always been a way of making a statement about the status of the building's owner, even if what goes on behind it is not very interesting. An imposing entrance in the Classical mode can be used effectively for a city hall, for the baronial building of a family-owned newspaper, or for an automobile showroom. Entrances to nineteenth-century houses were usually introduced by porches that might be composed according to the rules governing more monumental buildings or might be playfully assembled like embroidery.

The style that carried surface treatment as far as it could go originated in the eighteenth-century work of the Churriguera brothers, who came from a family of Barcelona sculptors known for lavishly carved altar retables. The brothers became architects and continued the family style of ornamentation, encrusting walls with fantasies in plaster and stone. Eventually, the name *Churrigueresque* became an umbrella for overwrought work in general and is often confused with the Plateresque, a sixteenth-century Spanish style that literally means "silversmithlike" and combined ornamental motifs from Gothic, Renaissance, and Moorish vocabularies. Both styles had little or nothing to do with the structure of buildings. The examples shown here illustrate the adaptability of this kind of ornament, which was often used in the 1920s to create pretentious entrances for rather plain buildings. Applied in relief form like brocaded wallpaper, Churrigueresque ornament could be easily produced by the running foot or yard.

106

107

108

109

110

111

The 1920s also drew on Mayan motifs popularized by the archaeological expeditions to the Yucatán. The Mayan Revival generally emphasized the continuous or allover character of the original reliefs and was used to enliven wall surfaces in much the same way as Churrigueresque was used, although the lower and more linear Mayanesque reliefs maintained the integrity of the wall plane. As seen when comparing figure 109 with figure 110, there is a striking recurrence throughout this period of forms that could be either watery or plantlike.

A preoccupation with natural forces runs through the whole history of ornament, although different formal means are used to express them. Unfortunately, we rarely know whether or not the meaning of the decorative forms we see played any role in their use. Take, for example, the doorway in figure 111. Was it the designer's intention to zap us with rays from a mysterious source? Or are these the tops of drapes that are pulled back to hang in vertical folds on either side of the door?

The apartment house doorway that features two ladies with voluted bosoms is obviously an architectural joke (figure 112). The other entrance employs towerlike elements that were commonly used for everything from salt shakers to gasoline pumps (figure 113).

The two examples of doorways from the Modern period, one designed by Frank Lloyd Wright in 1948 (figure 115), the other by Skidmore Owings and Merrill (SOM) in 1987 (figure 114), bring us to the period of nonfigurative detail. Wright was a master of detail and, over his long career, presided over stylistic change. Although he stylized hollyhocks in the 1920s for his famous house for Aline Barnsdall in Los Angeles, in the late 1940s he used unadorned brick just as expressively for the V. C. Morris Store in San Francisco. The largely blank facade has a zipperlike line of projecting bricks descending from the upper left corner of the facade down to mark a single red square inscribed with Wright's initials embedded in the wall to the left of the entrance.

Few architects are so daring as to sign their clients' buildings. The SOM architects who designed the building represented by the doorway in figure 114 also used the motif of a square, but in this case it is simply an accent like sequins on a gown, not a signature detail. This, the last, and most contemporary, example of architectural detail, displays several reversals of the traditional ways of making an entrance grand. The most obvious is the use of a clear, square pane of glass wider than the doors below, instead of an elaborate composition replete with symbols of authority set over the doorway. As yet, this building, like many others, is only identifiable by number. If, at some future date, it acquires great prestige as an address, an appropriate emblem may be created to fill the void. The blank shields on the Classical buildings described earlier seem to have been awaiting this kind of development.

112

113

114

115

Most contemporary buildings do not display inspirational symbols or inscriptions. Rarely do they express structure poetically. Architects of so-called Post-Modern buildings that allude to historic styles and in many cases incorporate classic elements as recognizable quotations from the past intended, as one of their goals, to engage viewers in a conversation about the building. But Post-Modernism appears to have exhausted its chosen store of architectural references. The conversation is boring. What was thought to be an appropriate heading for a new era is revealed as a style with the usual capacity of a style to spawn a vernacular or common language with greater value as commodity than as symbol. In these times of pluralism, it is too much to hope for the kind of consensus in architecture that created the long reign of the Classical vocabulary of detail. Still, a strong public interest in some new form of meaningful ornament may generate a new vocabulary of timely and topical detail that will renew the conversation.

116

BIBLIOGRAPHY

Byrne, Jane S. *Renaissance Ornament, Prints and Drawings.* New York: Metropolitan Museum of Art, 1981.

Campbell, Joseph. *The Mythic Image.* Princeton: Princeton University Press, 1974.

Cirlot, J. E. *A Dictionary of Symbols.* New York: Philosophical Library, 1971.

Cooper, J. C. *An Illustrated Encyclopedia of Traditional Symbols.* London: Thames & Hudson, 1978.

Evans, Joan. *Pattern, A Study of Ornament in Western Europe, 1180–1900.* New York: Da Capo Press, 1976.

Hersey, George. *The Lost Meaning of Classical Architecture.* Cambridge: MIT Press, 1988.

Jones, Owen. *The Grammar of Ornament.* London: Studio Editions, 1986.

Keswick, Maggie. *The Chinese Garden.* New York: St. Martin's Press, 1986.

Lewis, Philipa, and Gillian Darley. *Dictionary of Ornament.* New York: Pantheon, 1986.

Lurker, Manfred. *Dictionary of Gods and Goddesses, Devils and Demons.* New York: Routledge & Kegan Paul, 1987.

Princeton Architectural Press. *Canon. The Princeton Journal* Thematic Studies in Architecture. Princeton Journal 3.

Reed, Henry Hope. *The Golden City.* New York: W. W. Norton, 1971.

Tzonis, Alexander, and Liane Lefaivre. *Classical Architecture, the Poetics of Order.* Cambridge: MIT Press, 1987.

Vidler, Anthony. *The Writing of the Walls.* Princeton: Princeton Architectural Press, 1987.

Williams, C. A. S. *Outlines of Chinese Symbolism & Art Motives.* Mineola, New York: Dover, 1976.

INDEX

The locations of all photographic illustrations are San Francisco, California except where noted.